UNITE...
KINGDOM

Travel Guide 2025

The Ultimate Companion to Discover Great Britain's Rich History, Hidden Gems, and World-Famous Attractions.

ALFRED N. VINCENT

TABLE OF CONTENTS

Scan to View Map
UNITED KINGDOM

INTRODUCTION

Welcome to the United Kingdom a land of vibrant cities, breathtaking landscapes, and a rich history that spans centuries. The UK is where old-world charm meets modern-day energy, creating a travel experience unlike any other. From the iconic spires of Westminster Abbey to the vast, windswept hills of the Scottish Highlands, this is a place that invites you to explore, discover, and immerse yourself in its unique character. The rhythm of the UK is set by its bustling urban streets, its scenic countryside, and its cultural heritage, all blending in a dynamic atmosphere that beckons you to be a part of it. Whether you're visiting for a weekend getaway or a longer journey, the UK's charm will captivate you at every turn.

Why Visit the UK?

Why should the United Kingdom be at the top of your travel bucket list? Because it offers a truly diverse experience that will leave you with memories to last a lifetime. The UK is steeped in history, with landmarks like the majestic Tower of London, the ancient Stonehenge, and the regal Buckingham Palace offering a glimpse into the country's past. Yet, the UK is also a place where the present is just as exciting. From the cosmopolitan vibe of London's West End to the cultural festivals in Edinburgh and Cardiff, the UK thrives on creativity and modern energy.

Nature lovers will be equally enchanted by the beauty of the UK's countryside. Picture yourself walking through the Lake District's serene waters, exploring the rugged cliffs of Cornwall, or hiking in the Scottish Highlands, where the landscapes seem to go on forever. Every corner of the UK offers something new, from charming villages and historic castles to lively city streets and peaceful parks. With its incredible mix of history, culture, food, and nature, the UK is truly a top-tier destination for any traveler.

How to Use This Guide

This guide is your ultimate travel companion for experiencing the very best of the United Kingdom. It's designed to make your journey as easy and enjoyable as possible, providing you with all the essential information, insider tips, and ready-to-use itineraries you need. You'll find practical advice on everything from how to get around the UK, where to stay, and what to eat, to more detailed sections on the must-see cities, hidden gems, and the best ways to immerse yourself in British culture.

Each chapter is organized to help you get the most out of your time in the UK. From the first chapter on planning your trip to the last chapter offering sample itineraries for different types of travelers, we've included all the details you'll need to have a smooth and memorable experience. With tips on how to avoid tourist traps, recommended apps, and budget-saving hacks, you'll be well-prepared to explore like a local. This guide will not only help you navigate the UK's main attractions but also help you discover its hidden gems, making sure every part of your trip feels fresh, exciting, and unique.

PLANNING YOUR TRIP

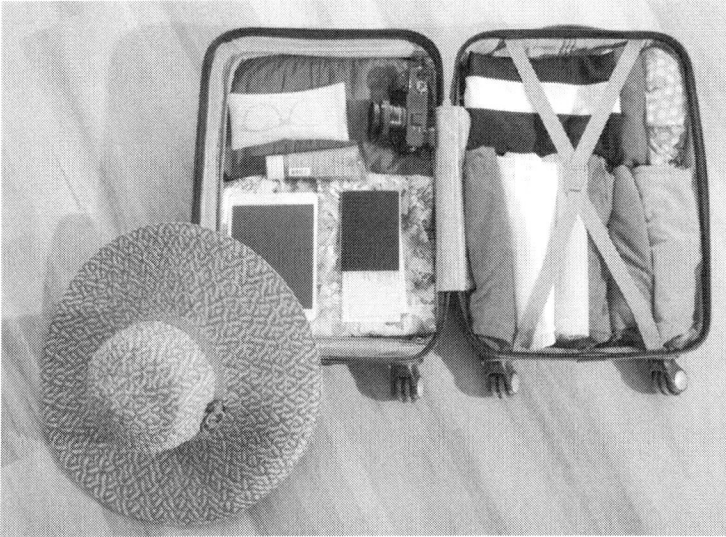

Best Time to Visit the United Kingdom

The United Kingdom is a year-round destination, each season offering a unique experience. However, the best time to visit depends on your preferences for weather, crowd sizes, and specific events. Let's break down what you can expect throughout the year:

Spring (March to May):

Spring brings milder weather and fewer crowds, making it an ideal time to visit. You can enjoy the blooming gardens, especially during events like the Chelsea Flower Show (late May), which draws visitors from around the world to see spectacular floral displays. The weather is unpredictable, so pack layers, a waterproof jacket, and comfortable shoes for walking. Temperatures typically range from 8°C to 15°C (46°F to 59°F).

Summer (June to August):

Summer is the peak tourist season in the UK, with warmer temperatures and long days (up to 16 hours of daylight in some parts). Expect higher hotel rates and larger crowds, particularly in major cities like London, Edinburgh, and Cardiff. Popular events include the Edinburgh Festival Fringe (August), the world's largest arts festival, and the

Glastonbury Festival (late June). The average temperature ranges from 15°C to 20°C (59°F to 68°F), but occasional heatwaves can push it higher. Be sure to book accommodations well in advance and pack light, breathable clothing along with good sunscreen.

Autumn (September to November):

Autumn is a fantastic time to visit, as the weather is still mild, and the changing foliage provides breathtaking scenery, especially in the Lake District and Scottish Highlands. Fewer tourists visit in autumn, so you can enjoy popular spots without the summer crowds. This season also hosts several festivals like the London Design Festival (September). Temperatures range from 10°C to 15°C (50°F to 59°F), so bring a warm jacket and layers, but it's usually too early for heavy winter clothing.

Winter (December to February):

Winter in the UK is cold, with temperatures often dipping below 0°C (32°F), especially in northern areas. The weather is damp, with rain and occasional snow. This is a great time to visit if you enjoy winter festivals, Christmas markets (like those in Bath, Edinburgh, and London's Winter Wonderland), and cozying up by the fire in a pub. However, be prepared for shorter days, with only around 7 to 8 hours of daylight. The average temperature ranges from 1°C to 8°C (34°F to 46°F). Warm layers, a waterproof jacket, and boots are essential.

How Long Should You Stay?

How much time should you spend in the UK? That depends on how much of the country you want to see. Here are some suggestions for various trip durations:

3 Days (Perfect for a short getaway to London):

- Day 1: Visit iconic attractions such as the Tower of London, Buckingham Palace, and Westminster Abbey.

- Day 2: Explore cultural sites like the British Museum, and Tate Modern, and enjoy shopping in Covent Garden.

- Day 3: Take a day trip to nearby destinations like Stonehenge or Oxford.

7 Days (For first-time visitors wanting to explore a variety of cities):

- Days 1-3: Explore London, including museums, parks, and a day trip to Windsor or Greenwich.

- Day 4-5: Take a train to Edinburgh, spending time in the Royal Mile, Edinburgh Castle, and Arthur's Seat.

- Day 6-7: Visit Cardiff, and enjoy the Cardiff Castle and Bute Park, or travel to the Cotswolds for a rural escape.

10+ Days (For an in-depth UK exploration):

Days 1-4: London exploration, including markets, neighborhoods like Notting Hill, and museums.

- Days 5-7: Edinburgh and the surrounding Scottish Highlands, visiting Loch Ness and the Isle of Skye.
- Days 8-10+: Spend time in Wales, touring Cardiff, hiking Snowdonia, and discovering the Brecon Beacons. Alternatively, embark on an extensive road trip through Cornwall, Lake District, and Yorkshire.

Essential Travel Documents and Visa Information

Before heading to the UK, ensure you have the necessary documents for entry. For most visitors, this means a valid passport, and in some cases, a visa.

Passport Validity: Your passport should be valid for at least 6 months beyond your intended stay in the UK.

- Visa Requirements: Citizens from the EU, EEA, and Switzerland do not require a visa for short stays. Citizens from other countries, including the US, Canada, and Australia, typically do not need a visa for stays of up to 6 months for tourism. However, travelers from certain countries may require a Standard Visitor Visa.

To apply for a visa, follow these general steps:

- Visit the official UK government website at gov.uk/standard-visitor-visa.
- Complete the online application and provide the necessary documents (passport, travel plans, proof of funds).
- Schedule an appointment at your nearest visa center for biometrics and submission of documents.
- Pay the visa fee (usually around £95 for a 6-month visitor visa).

- Wait for processing, which can take anywhere from 3 to 12 weeks, depending on the country.
- Tip: Be sure to apply early to avoid processing delays, especially during peak travel seasons.

Packing Tips

The UK's weather can be unpredictable, so packing appropriately is crucial. Here's a breakdown for each season:

- Spring: Layering is key. Pack a light jacket, sweater, and an umbrella for the occasional rain. Comfortable walking shoes are essential for sightseeing.
- Summer: While temperatures are generally mild, you may encounter heatwaves. Bring light clothing, sunscreen, and a hat for sun protection. A

waterproof jacket is still recommended, as rain is frequent.

- Autumn: Bring warm layers, scarves, and a waterproof jacket. Comfortable hiking shoes are ideal for exploring nature.

- Winter: Pack a heavy coat, gloves, hat, and waterproof boots. You'll also want to bring an umbrella, as winter can be wet and cold.

Additional essentials:

- Adapters: The UK uses Type G electrical outlets, so bring the proper adapter for your devices.

- Medications: If you take any medications, bring them in their original packaging along with a prescription.

- Travel Guide/Maps: Though many places in the UK have great mobile apps, a physical map or guidebook can still come in handy, especially in rural areas.

Currency and Budgeting Tips

The UK uses the Pound Sterling (GBP). Here's a breakdown of what to expect:

- Currency: Credit and debit cards are widely accepted in cities and most rural areas, but it's advisable to carry some cash for smaller purchases or in more remote areas.

- Tipping: Tipping is appreciated but not mandatory. In restaurants, it's customary to leave a tip of 10-15%, though many places include a service charge. For taxis, rounding up the fare is common.

Budgeting:

- Average meal price: £10–£20 per person at casual restaurants.

- Museum entry fees: Many national museums are free (e.g., British Museum), but some special exhibitions or galleries may charge (£10–£25).

- Public transport: Consider purchasing an Oyster Card in London for discounts on buses, trains, and the Underground. A weekly Travelcard is also a good option for regular use.

Budget-saving tips:

- Free Attractions: Take advantage of free entry to museums, parks, and many historical sites in London and other cities.

- Discounted Travel: Use railcards or online booking services like Trainline to get discounted train tickets.

Health and Safety

Before traveling, here are key health and safety considerations:

- Travel Insurance: Always purchase comprehensive travel insurance that covers medical emergencies, trip cancellations, and lost luggage.

- Emergency Number: The emergency number for police, fire, or medical emergencies is 999.

- Public Transport Safety: While the UK is generally safe, busy stations or buses can attract pickpockets. Keep your belongings secure, especially in crowded areas like London's Oxford Street.

- Health Precautions: The UK has excellent healthcare, but it's recommended to check your health insurance coverage for medical expenses abroad. If you're from the EU, ensure your EHIC card is valid.

- Apps: Download transportation apps like Citymapper for navigation or National Rail for train schedules.

- While traveling, always stay aware of your surroundings, avoid poorly lit areas at night, and be cautious when accepting unsolicited offers from street vendors.

GETTING AROUND THE UK

Navigating the UK

The United Kingdom offers a variety of transportation options that cater to both urban and rural travelers. From fast and efficient public transport in cities to scenic countryside routes, getting around the UK is both easy and diverse. Here's a breakdown of your options:

- Public Transport: The UK boasts an extensive network of trains, buses, and ferries. Major cities like London, Manchester, Edinburgh, and Cardiff are well-connected, offering reliable and frequent services. Public transport is efficient, and you'll find that it's the most convenient and cost-effective way to explore cities and travel between towns.

- Trains: National Rail covers most long-distance travel between cities and towns. Regional train services connect smaller towns, while high-speed trains like the Eurostar link London with Paris and Brussels.

- Buses: For shorter journeys, buses are a great option. National coach services like National Express and Megabus offer long-distance travel across the UK, while local buses in cities operate at regular intervals.

- Ferries: For coastal destinations and islands like the Isle of Wight, Isles of Scilly, and Isle of Skye, ferries are an essential mode of transport. Many ferry routes connect cities to islands or other coastal locations.

- Tip: Travel passes like the BritRail Pass (for train travel across Britain) or local day passes (like the London Travelcard) can offer great discounts on transportation.

Trains, Buses, and the London Underground

Trains:

The UK has an efficient train network with a range of services:

- National Rail offers connections between major cities and towns. Visit National Rail for timetables, route maps, and ticket bookings.

- Key routes: The West Coast Main Line (London to Manchester, Glasgow), East Coast Main Line (London to Edinburgh), and the Great Western Railway (London to Bristol, Cardiff) are some of the busiest and most scenic.

- Ticket booking: You can book tickets via National Rail, Trainline (www.thetrainline.com), or directly from train providers. For cheaper fares, it's recommended to book tickets in advance (3-12 weeks ahead) to secure discounts.

Buses:

- National Express and Megabus are popular national coach services that run between major cities and towns. Both companies offer affordable fares, starting as low as £5 for early bookings.

- Local Buses: In cities like London, buses are a convenient option for short distances. You can pay via contactless card or mobile payments (using Apple Pay or Google Pay).

- Tip: Always check if your ticket allows unlimited travel within a day or zone, and if there's a discount for purchasing multi-ride passes.

London Underground (The Tube):

- The London Underground is one of the most iconic subway systems in the world, covering all of Greater London. It's efficient, fast, and easy to use, but navigating its complex network of lines and zones can be overwhelming for newcomers.

- Ticketing: Use an Oyster Card or contactless payment to travel on the Tube, buses, and even some trains. The Visitor Oyster Card offers discounts and is available for tourists. A single journey on the Tube starts at £2.40, depending on the distance traveled.

- Peak vs Off-Peak: Avoid traveling during rush hours (8:00 AM - 9:30 AM and 5:00 PM - 6:30 PM) to avoid crowded trains. Off-peak fares are cheaper and more comfortable.

- Zone System: London is divided into 9 fare zones, with Zone 1 covering the city center and outer zones being cheaper. The cost of travel depends on which zones you enter.
- Tip: Use apps like Citymapper to navigate public transport routes, which provide live updates, train schedules, and walking directions.

Renting a Car and Exploring Off the Beaten Path

Renting a car in the UK allows you to explore hidden gems and picturesque locations that are inaccessible by public transport. Whether it's the rolling hills of the Cotswolds or the dramatic cliffs of Cornwall, renting a car is an excellent option for adventure.

Renting a Car:

- Age Requirements: Renters usually need to be at least 21 years old, although some agencies may require you to be 25. Drivers under 25 might face an additional young driver fee.

- Insurance: Make sure to get comprehensive insurance, covering third-party liability, theft, and damage. Always review the excess (deductible) fees before confirming the rental.

- Driving Regulations: The UK drives on the left side of the road, and cars are right-hand drive. Be sure to familiarize yourself with road signs and regulations before getting on the road. Speed limits vary from

30 mph in urban areas to 60 mph on single-lane rural roads and 70 mph on motorways.

Scenic Drives:

- Lake District: Explore England's most beautiful countryside with winding roads, quaint villages, and serene lakes. Consider stopping in Keswick or Ambleside for a peaceful retreat.

- Cornwall: Drive the coastal roads of Cornwall, passing through charming fishing villages and along rugged cliffs. A highlight is the scenic B3306 from St. Ives to Land's End.

- North Coast 500 (Scotland): This is a famous circular route around the Scottish Highlands, covering Inverness, John O'Groats, and remote seaside villages.

Car Rental Agencies:

- Hertz (www.hertz.co.uk)

- Enterprise (www.enterprise.co.uk)

- Tip: Make sure to book your rental car in advance to secure the best rates, especially in high season.

The Best Travel Apps and Websites for Visitors

Navigating the UK is made easy with the right apps and websites. Here are some top recommendations:

- Trainline (www.thetrainline.com): Book train tickets across the UK with ease, and find discounts on fares.

- Citymapper (www.citymapper.com): A must-have app for navigating cities like London, Edinburgh, and Manchester. It gives real-time updates on bus, train, and tube routes.

- TfL Go (www.tfl.gov.uk): London's official transport website offers a wealth of information, including routes, timetables, and updates on disruptions.

- Google Maps: For offline navigation, use Google Maps, which provides live traffic updates and directions.

- Tip: Download maps and transport apps before your trip to avoid roaming charges and ensure smooth navigation even without internet access.

Tips for Easy Travel Between Cities and Regions

Traveling between cities and regions in the UK is simple, but there are a few key tips to make the journey easier and cheaper:

- Train Travel: The train is often the most convenient mode of transport between major cities. BritRail

Pass offers unlimited train travel for up to 8 days within 1 month. This is ideal for tourists wishing to explore different regions without buying individual tickets.

- Long-Distance Buses: National Express and Megabus offer affordable coach services between major cities. Fares can be as low as £5 if you book early.

- Air Travel: For longer distances (e.g., London to Edinburgh), budget airlines like easyJet and Ryanair provide affordable flights, although you'll need to factor in airport time.

- Regional Travel: Cities like York, Bath, and Oxford can be easily accessed by bus or train from London. For less accessible areas like the Scottish Highlands or rural Wales, it's best to plan and check schedules carefully.

- Tip: Booking in advance for trains and buses can save you significant money, especially for long-distance routes. Also, look into regional travel passes for convenience and savings.

TOP CITIES TO EXPLORE

London

Scan to View Map
LONDON

Tower of London

- Address: Tower Hill, London EC3N 4AB

- Opening Hours: Daily, 9:00 AM – 5:30 PM

- Entry Fees: £29.90 for adults, £14.90 for children (5-15 years old)

- What to Expect: The Tower of London is one of the most famous landmarks in the UK, housing the Crown Jewels and centuries of history. Don't miss the iconic Beefeaters (Yeoman Warders) guiding tours and telling fascinating stories of royal history. Try to visit early in the day to avoid crowds, particularly if you want to see the Crown Jewels up close.

- Tickets: Pre-book tickets online at www.hrp.org.uk for a discount.

Buckingham Palace

- Address: Buckingham Palace Road, London SW1A 1AA

- Changing of the Guard: 11:00 AM daily (times may vary, so check the schedule).

- What to Expect: The iconic Changing of the Guard ceremony is a must-see event, with soldiers in their famous red tunics and bearskin hats. For a deeper dive into royal history, you can book a tour of the State Rooms during summer when the palace is open to the public.

- Tickets: Summer tours are available at £30 for adults and £16 for children. Book in advance at www.rct.uk.

Westminster Abbey

- Address: 20 Deans Yard, Westminster, London SW1P 3PA

- Opening Hours: Monday – Saturday, 9:30 AM – 3:30 PM (closed on Sundays except for services)

- Entry Fees: £23 for adults, £10 for children

- What to Expect: A UNESCO World Heritage site and the traditional site for British royal coronations. Don't miss the tombs of monarchs, poets, and scientists. You can also book a guided tour for a deeper understanding of the abbey's history.

- Tickets: Book online at www.westminster-abbey.org for discounts.

Covent Garden

- Address: Covent Garden, London WC2E 8RF

- What to Explore: Known for its street performers and artisanal markets, Covent Garden is a vibrant area filled with cafes, boutique shops, and unique performers. It's a great place to soak in the local atmosphere and watch a spontaneous performance or two.

- Best Time to Visit: Afternoon and evenings for the best street performances.

Notting Hill

- Notable Spots: The colorful houses, Portobello Road Market, and the Notting Hill Carnival (if visiting in August). This trendy neighborhood is a favorite for Instagram-worthy shots and shopping.

- What Makes It Unique: A laid-back charm with local markets, antique shops, and quaint cafes. Don't miss out on browsing through Portobello Road Market for vintage items and fresh produce.

South Bank

- Address: South Bank, London SE1
- What to Explore: Along the River Thames, this area is home to iconic cultural attractions such as the London Eye, National Theatre, and Tate Modern. Walk along the riverbanks and enjoy the lively atmosphere, with many street food vendors, public art installations, and stunning views of the city skyline.

- Best Time to Visit: Late afternoon for views of the sunset over the Thames and to avoid crowds.

Edinburgh

Iconic Attractions

Edinburgh Castle

- Address: Castlehill, Edinburgh EH1 2NG

- Opening Hours: Daily, 9:30 AM – 5:00 PM

- Entry Fees: £19.50 for adults, £11.50 for children

- What to Expect: Perched on a dormant volcano, Edinburgh Castle offers sweeping views of the city. Explore its museums, the Crown Jewels, and the Stone of Destiny (used in royal coronations). If visiting during the summer, arrive early to avoid the crowds.

- Tickets: Purchase online at www.edinburghcastle.scot for discounts and to skip the line.

Royal Mile

- What to Explore: This historic street stretches from Edinburgh Castle to Holyrood Palace. Along the way, you'll encounter old closes (alleys), historic buildings, and vibrant shops. Notable spots include St Giles' Cathedral and The Real Mary King's Close, an underground tour of Edinburgh's hidden history.

- Best Time to Visit: Morning or early afternoon for fewer crowds and to catch some street performances.

Arthur's Seat

- Address: Holyrood Park, Edinburgh

- What to Expect: A hike up this dormant volcano offers panoramic views of the city, including the Firth of Forth and the surrounding hills. The walk is free, but it's important to wear sturdy shoes and bring water, especially if hiking in the warmer months.

- Tips: For an easier route, take the Crags path to enjoy scenic views along the way.

Unique Neighborhoods and Festivals

Old Town and New Town

- Old Town: Known for its medieval buildings, narrow streets, and the iconic Grassmarket area.

Explore the Edinburgh Vaults and National Museum of Scotland.

- New Town: A neoclassical architectural marvel with wide streets and Georgian buildings. Don't miss Princess Street Gardens and shopping along George Street.

Edinburgh Festival Fringe:

- Dates: August (usually the first three weeks of the month)

- What to Expect: The world's largest arts festival, with thousands of performances across all genres. Be sure to book tickets in advance, as shows sell out quickly.

Cardiff

Iconic Attractions

Cardiff Castle

- Address: Castle Street, Cardiff CF10 3RB

- Opening Hours: Daily, 9:00 AM – 5:00 PM

- Entry Fees: £14 for adults, £10 for children

- What to Expect: A medieval castle with a rich history, Cardiff Castle offers a fascinating glimpse into Wales' past. Explore the castle's keep, the opulent interiors, and the Firing Line museum, showcasing Welsh military history.

- Tickets: Available at www.cardiffcastle.com.

Bute Park

- Address: North Road, Cardiff CF10 3DX

- What to Explore: This beautiful park is perfect for walking or relaxing in nature. It's especially vibrant in spring and summer when the flowers are in bloom. Explore the park's trails, or take a stroll along the river.

- Best Time to Visit: Late spring and summer for lush greenery.

National Museum Wales

- Address: Cathays Park, Cardiff CF10 3NP

- Opening Hours: Tuesday – Sunday, 10:00 AM – 5:00 PM

- Entry Fees: Free (some special exhibitions may charge)

- What to Expect: Home to an impressive collection of art, archaeology, and natural history. Don't miss the extensive collection of Impressionist paintings.

Unique Neighborhoods and Experiences

Cardiff Bay

- What to Explore: A revitalized waterfront area with a lively atmosphere. Visit Techniquest (a hands-on science museum), dine at the Pierhead Building, or enjoy a walk along Bute Park. For nightlife, head to the Senedd or Millennium Centre for arts and performance venues.
- Best Time to Visit: Evening for vibrant nightlife and scenic views of the bay.

Belfast

Scan to View Map
BELFAST

Iconic Attractions

Titanic Quarter

- Address: Titanic Quarter, Belfast BT3 9EP

- Opening Hours: Daily, 10:00 AM – 5:00 PM

- Entry Fees: £19 for adults, £9 for children

- What to Expect: A modern complex housing the Titanic Belfast museum, which tells the story of the ill-fated ship. The area also includes SS Nomadic and Titanic Dock.

- Tickets: Book in advance at www.titanicbelfast.com.

Giant's Causeway

- Address: Bushmills, County Antrim BT57 8SU

- What to Expect: A UNESCO World Heritage site, famous for its unique hexagonal rock formations. Explore the coastline, or visit the Visitor Centre for more information.

- Entry Fees: £13 for adults, £6 for children

- Tip: Avoid peak times (summer weekends) for a more peaceful visit.

Local Culture and Hidden Gems

Cathedral Quarter

- What to Explore: Known for its vibrant pub scene, art galleries, and street murals, this area is where Belfast's history and culture collide. Be sure to check out St. Anne's Cathedral and enjoy a pint at the iconic Duke of York pub.

- Best Time to Visit: Late afternoon and evening to experience the lively atmosphere and enjoy dinner in one of the many local eateries.

DISCOVERING THE COUNTRYSIDE

AND NATURE

Exploring England's Lake District and Peak District

Lake District

The Lake District in northern England is one of the UK's most beloved natural gems, renowned for its stunning lakes, rugged mountains, and quaint villages. Whether you're hiking, boating, or simply soaking in the views, there's plenty to explore.

Windermere

The largest lake in England, Windermere offers excellent boat tours, and you can explore the surrounding area with several scenic walking routes. Don't miss the Bowness-on-Windermere village for lakeside cafes and shops. Walking routes such as the Orrest Head offer panoramic views. Best visited in spring or autumn to avoid crowds.

- Address: Windermere, LA23 1BB
- Boat Tours: Windermere Lake Cruises, www.windermere-lakecruises.co.uk

Keswick

A charming town nestled by Derwentwater, Keswick is ideal for hiking and outdoor activities. Popular routes include the Catbells hike, which offers great views of the lake. While there, explore the Keswick Museum and Art Gallery or stroll around the Market Square.

- Address: Keswick, CA12 5DG
- Hike: Catbells, easy to moderate, great for beginners.

Peak District

The Peak District is the UK's first national park, offering an array of picturesque valleys, hills, and historical sites. It's a prime location for hiking, cycling, and exploring medieval towns.

Dovedale

Famous for its stepping stones across the River Dove, this area is perfect for gentle walks or picnics by the river. It's an excellent spot for families.

- Address: Dovedale, Ashbourne DE6 2AY

- Walk: Easy walking route to the famous stepping
  stones.

Mam Tor

Known as the "Shivering Mountain," this peak is a popular
hiking destination offering breathtaking views of the Peak
District. The Mam Tor Circular is a classic walk that offers
panoramic vistas of the surrounding landscape.

- Address: Mam Tor, Castleton, Hope Valley S33
  8WA

- Walk: Moderate hike, 2-3 hours, stunning views at
  the top.

Hiking in the Scottish Highlands

The Scottish Highlands are a haven for hiking enthusiasts,
offering towering mountains, lush valleys, and some of the

best views in the UK. Here's a guide to some of the region's top hiking spots.

Ben Nevis

As the highest mountain in the UK, Ben Nevis is a must for avid hikers. The Mountain Path is the most popular route, though it's quite strenuous. During the summer months, this is a popular trek, so start early to avoid the crowds.

- Address: Ben Nevis, Fort William PH33 6SY
- Hike: Mountain Path – challenging, takes around 7-8 hours.

Glencoe

Known for its dramatic landscapes, Glencoe offers various hiking routes, including the iconic Three Sisters trail, where you'll experience some of Scotland's most rugged scenery.

A must-see is the Lost Valley Walk, a moderate trail with incredible views.

- Address: Glencoe, Ballachulish PH49 4HX
- Hike: Three Sisters – moderate to challenging.

Cairngorms National Park

For a diverse range of landscapes, head to Cairngorms National Park, where you can find a range of hiking trails, from easy lakeside strolls to challenging mountain ascents. Wildlife watching is also a highlight, with opportunities to see red deer and golden eagles.

- Address: Aviemore, PH22 1QD
- Hike: Cairn Gorm Summit – challenging.

COASTAL BEAUTY

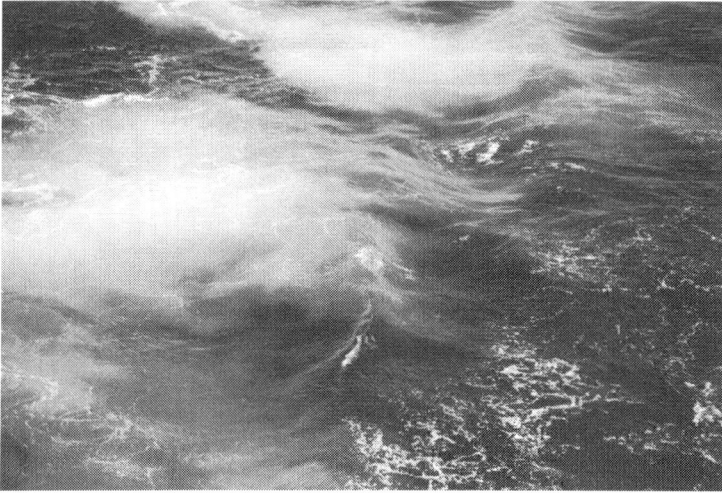

Cornwall

Cornwall offers some of the most breathtaking coastal views in the UK, with stunning beaches, rugged cliffs, and charming villages.

St Ives

Known for its golden sandy beaches and thriving arts scene, St Ives is a great place for both relaxation and exploration. Visit Tate St Ives for contemporary art or walk around the cobbled streets lined with galleries.

- Address: St Ives, TR26 1AF
- Best Time to Visit: Spring and early autumn for fewer tourists.

Penzance

This seaside town has historical landmarks like Morrab Gardens and offers easy access to Land's End, the southwesternmost point of England. The South West Coast Path provides stunning views of the cliffs and ocean.

- Address: Penzance, TR18 4HG
- Nearby Attraction: Land's End, TR19 7AA.

Devon

With its coastal cliffs and sandy beaches, Devon is perfect for nature lovers and those looking for coastal walks.

Jurassic Coast

A UNESCO World Heritage Site, the Jurassic Coast is famous for fossil hunting. Lyme Regis is particularly popular for its fossil beaches. Don't miss the Durdle Door limestone arch and Lulworth Cove.

- Address: Lyme Regis, DT7 3JJ
- Fossil Hunting: Best at low tide, wear sturdy footwear.

Wales

Wales is home to dramatic coastlines, with towering cliffs and pristine beaches.

Pembrokeshire

Famous for its rugged coastline and Pembrokeshire Coast Path, this area is ideal for hiking and beach activities. St

Davids, the UK's smallest city, is a great base for exploring the area.

- Address: Pembrokeshire, SA62 6SD
- Walk: Pembrokeshire Coast Path, a scenic 186-mile route.

National Parks to Visit

Snowdonia National Park

Snowdonia offers a perfect blend of rugged mountains, serene lakes, and charming villages.

Mount Snowdon

One of the UK's most popular hikes, Mount Snowdon offers several routes to the summit, with the Llanberis Path being the easiest. For a less crowded experience, consider the Snowdon Ranger Path.

- Address: Llanberis, Caernarfon LL55 4UL

- Hike: Llanberis Path – moderate, 6-7 hours.

Betws-y-Coed

This picturesque village is ideal for exploring the surrounding woodlands and waterfalls. The Swallow Falls is a popular attraction nearby.

- Address: Betws-y-Coed, LL24 0AS
- Hike: Swallow Falls, an easy walk.

Dartmoor National Park

Dartmoor is a vast expanse of wild moorland, granite tors, and ancient villages.

Widecombe-in-the-Moor

A quaint village surrounded by scenic walking trails, including the route to Haytor Rocks, a famous granite tor offering spectacular views of the moorland.

- Address: Widecombe-in-the-Moor, TQ13 7TA

- Hike: Haytor Rocks, moderate hike.

The Isle of Skye is famous for its dramatic landscapes and mystical atmosphere.

Old Man of Storr

A must-hike for anyone visiting Skye, this rocky pinnacle offers breathtaking views of the island and is accessible via a short but steep hike.

- Address: Old Man of Storr, Portree, IV51 9HX

- Hike: Old Man of Storr – moderate.

UK'S RICH HISTORY AND

CULTURAL HERITAGE

Ancient Monuments and Historic Sites

Stonehenge

One of the UK's most iconic landmarks, Stonehenge is a

prehistoric monument that continues to captivate visitors

with its mysterious origins. Situated in Wiltshire, this ancient site dates back over 5,000 years.

- Address: Amesbury, Salisbury SP4 7DE

- Opening Hours: Typically 9:30 AM - 5:00 PM (varies by season)

- Entry Fees: Adult £21.10, Children £12.60, Family (2 adults, 2 children) £55.60

- Getting There: The nearest train station is Salisbury (about 9 miles away), with shuttle buses available to the site. Alternatively, car rentals or guided tours are common options.

- Tips for Visiting: To avoid the busiest times, visit early in the morning or later in the afternoon. For a more in-depth experience, book a guided tour or use the audio guide, which explains the site's significance and history.

Hadrian's Wall

Hadrian's Wall stretches 73 miles across northern England and is a UNESCO World Heritage site, originally built by the Romans to protect their empire. The wall and its forts provide fascinating insights into Roman life in Britain.

- Key Sites: Vindolanda (a Roman fort near Hexham) and Housesteads Roman Fort are among the best-preserved areas.

- Hiking: Various walking routes follow sections of the wall, ranging from easy walks to challenging treks. The Hadrian's Wall Path National Trail is a great way to experience the site.

- Entry Fees: Fees vary by site, with most forts charging around £7-£9 for entry.

- Tips for Visiting: Wear sturdy shoes and bring water, especially if walking the trail. Consider booking a guided tour for historical insights and to enhance your experience.

Roman Baths

Located in the historic city of Bath, the Roman Baths offer a glimpse into life during Roman Britain. Visitors can explore the ancient baths and museum, showcasing Roman artifacts.

- Address: Stall Street, Bath BA1 1LZ

- Opening Hours: 9:00 AM - 6:00 PM (varies by season)

- Entry Fees: Adult £25.00, Children £11.00, Family £62.00

- Tips for Visiting: To avoid crowds, visit early or late in the day, especially during the summer months. Don't miss the stunning Great Bath and the

Sacred Spring. Nearby, you can also explore the Pump Room for afternoon tea or a spa experience.

Castles and Palaces

Windsor Castle

The oldest and largest inhabited castle in the world, Windsor Castle is the official residence of the British royal family. It is a symbol of the monarchy and boasts a rich history dating back over 1,000 years.

- Address: Windsor, SL4 1NJ

- Opening Hours: 10:00 AM - 5:15 PM (varies by season)

- Entry Fees: Adult £23.50, Children £13.50, Family £59.00

- Must-See: St George's Chapel (where many royal weddings are held) and the State Apartments.

- Tips for Visiting: Arrive early to explore the castle grounds and gardens before crowds arrive. It's best to visit during the off-season (autumn or spring) to avoid the summer rush. Tickets can be booked online to skip the line.

Edinburgh Castle

Perched on an extinct volcanic hill, Edinburgh Castle is Scotland's most visited paid tourist attraction. It offers sweeping views over the city and is home to the Crown Jewels of Scotland and the Stone of Destiny.

- Address: Castlehill, Edinburgh EH1 2NG

- Opening Hours: 9:30 AM - 6:00 PM (varies by season)

- Entry Fees: Adult £19.50, Children £11.50

- Must-See: The Crown Jewels, St Margaret's Chapel, and National War Museum.

- Tips for Visiting: Book tickets online to avoid long queues, and consider visiting in the morning for a quieter experience. The Esplanade and Royal Mile leading up to the castle are also worth exploring.

Other Notable Castles

- Tower of London: Address: London, EC3N 4AB | Entry Fees: Adult £29.90, Children £14.90 | Explore the Crown Jewels and the White Tower.

- Stirling Castle: Address: Stirling, FK8 1EJ | Entry Fees: Adult £16.50, Children £9.50 | A key site in Scottish history, with stunning views over the surrounding area.

- Warwick Castle: Address: Warwick, CV34 6AH | Entry Fees: Adult £24.50, Children £18.50 | Known for its medieval reenactments and interactive exhibits.

Museums and Art Galleries

British Museum

One of the world's greatest museums, the British Museum houses a vast collection of artifacts from across the globe, including the famous Rosetta Stone and Egyptian mummies.

- Address: Great Russell Street, London WC1B 3DG
- Opening Hours: 10:00 AM - 5:30 PM

- Entry Fees: Free (special exhibitions may charge)

- Must-See: The Rosetta Stone, Parthenon Marbles, and Egyptian Galleries.

- Tips for Visiting: The museum can be overwhelming due to its size, so plan ahead and focus on specific exhibits. The museum offers free guided tours that are worth joining.

Tate Modern

Located on the South Bank of the Thames, Tate Modern is home to a stunning collection of modern and contemporary art from renowned artists like Picasso, Dali, and Warhol.

- Address: Bankside, London SE1 9TG

- Opening Hours: 10:00 AM - 6:00 PM

- Entry Fees: Free (special exhibitions may charge)

- Tips for Visiting: Tate Modern can be crowded, so visit during the week to avoid the weekend rush.

The Tate Exchange hosts interactive exhibits, and the Tate Café offers views of the Thames.

National Gallery

The National Gallery in London houses one of the world's finest collections of European paintings, featuring works by Van Gogh, Leonardo da Vinci, and Turner.

- Address: Trafalgar Square, London WC2N 5DN
- Opening Hours: 10:00 AM - 6:00 PM
- Entry Fees: Free (special exhibitions may charge)
- Must-See: The Arnolfini Portrait by Van Eyck, The Fighting Temeraire by Turner, and Madonna of the Rocks by Da Vinci.

Royal History and Traditions

Changing of the Guard

The Changing of the Guard at Buckingham Palace is one of London's most famous ceremonies. Watch the Household Cavalry and Foot Guards in their iconic red tunics and bearskin hats perform this historic tradition.

- Location: Buckingham Palace, London SW1A 1AA
- Timings: 11:30 AM daily (check the schedule as it varies by season)
- Tips for Seeing the Ceremony: Arrive early to secure a good viewing spot in front of the palace gates. Alternatively, Horse Guards Parade (Whitehall) also hosts a Changing of the Guard ceremony, with fewer crowds.

Buckingham Palace

The official residence of the British monarch, with the State Rooms open to visitors during the summer months.

- Opening Hours: Summer (dates vary), 9:30 AM - 6:30 PM
- Ticket Fees: Adult £27.00, Children £15.00

Sandringham and Balmoral

Summer residences of the royal family, located in Norfolk and the Scottish Highlands, respectively.

- Sandringham: Open to the public from April to October.
- Balmoral: Open to the public during the summer months.

FOOD, DRINK, AND LOCAL

DELIGHTS

Traditional British Dishes

Fish and Chips

No visit to the UK is complete without tasting the classic

fish and chips. The dish, consisting of battered fish (usually cod or haddock) and deep-fried chips, is a staple of British cuisine.

Where to Try:

The Magpie Café, Whitby: A renowned spot offering some of the best fish and chips in the UK. Try the mushy peas and tartar sauce to complete the meal.

- Address: 14-16 Pier Road, Whitby YO21 3PU
- Opening Hours: 11:00 AM - 8:00 PM
- Price: Fish and chips from £10.00

Poppies, London: A retro-inspired, award-winning fish and chips shop, serving up this iconic dish with flair.

- Address: 6-8 Hanbury Street, London E1 6QR
- Opening Hours: 12:00 PM - 10:00 PM
- Price: Fish and chips from £12.50

Harry Ramsden's, Various Locations: Famous for its crispy batter and freshly caught fish, Harry Ramsden's is a UK institution.

- Price: Fish and chips from £9.00
- Tip: For the full experience, try adding mushy peas or pickled onions. Don't forget the tartar sauce for dipping!

Roast Dinners

A British tradition, the Sunday roast features roasted meat (often beef, lamb, or chicken), Yorkshire pudding, roast potatoes, and seasonal vegetables. It's a hearty meal enjoyed across the UK, particularly on Sundays.

Where to Try:

The Albion, London: Known for its exceptional roast dinners and classic pub atmosphere.

- Address: 10-11 Chiswell Street, London EC1Y 4UQ

- Opening Hours: 12:00 PM - 9:00 PM

- Price: Roast dinners from £18.00

The Crown & Anchor, Oxford: A cozy spot serving top-notch Sunday roasts in a traditional setting.

- Address: 74 High Street, Oxford OX1 4BG

- Opening Hours: 12:00 PM - 8:00 PM

- Price: Roast dinners from £15.00

- Tip: Arrive early, as Sunday roasts are a popular meal. Be prepared for wait times, particularly during peak dining hours.

Other British Classics

- Shepherd's Pie: A savory meat pie made with minced lamb and vegetables, topped with mashed potatoes.

- Full English Breakfast: A hearty breakfast featuring sausages, bacon, eggs, beans, toast, and grilled tomatoes.

Exploring the World of Afternoon Tea

A quintessentially British tradition, afternoon tea involves light snacks, such as finger sandwiches, scones with clotted cream and jam, and a selection of teas. It began in the 19th century as a way to bridge the gap between lunch and dinner and has since evolved into a grand social event.

Where to Experience Afternoon Tea:

The Ritz, London: One of the most famous places to experience afternoon tea, with an elegant setting and impeccable service.

- Address: 150 Piccadilly, London W1J 9BR
- Opening Hours: 12:30 PM - 4:30 PM
- Price: £65.00 per person
- Booking Tips: Book well in advance, especially for weekends. A smart dress code is required.

Bettys Café Tea Rooms, York: A delightful spot offering a traditional afternoon tea in an iconic setting.

- Address: 6-8 St. Helen's Square, York YO1 8QP
- Opening Hours: 9:00 AM - 6:00 PM
- Price: Afternoon tea from £21.95
- Tip: Booking is essential, especially during the tourist season.

Claridge's, London: Known for its classic afternoon tea, served in a luxurious environment.

- Address: Brook Street, London W1K 4HR
- Opening Hours: 1:00 PM - 5:00 PM
- Price: £60.00 per person
- Booking Tips: Dress smartly, and make a reservation ahead of time to secure a spot.

Pub Culture

The British pub is more than just a place to drink; it's a social hub for the community. Pubs often serve a variety of local ales, ciders, and lagers, along with traditional pub food like pies, fish and chips, and hearty stews.

Where to Try:

The Eagle & Child, Oxford: Famous for being the meeting place of literary figures J.R.R. Tolkien and C.S. Lewis.

- Address: 49 St Giles', Oxford OX1 3LU
- Opening Hours: 11:00 AM - 11:00 PM
- Tip: Stop by for a pint and soak in the historic atmosphere.

The George Inn, London: A historic pub located near Southwark Cathedral.

- Address: 77 Borough High Street, London SE1 1NH

- Opening Hours: 12:00 PM - 11:00 PM

- Tip: Enjoy the charming atmosphere, especially in the courtyard.

The Old Swan, Harrogate: A historic pub with a beautiful interior and exceptional local ales.

- Address: Swan Road, Harrogate HG1 2SA

- Opening Hours: 11:00 AM - 11:00 PM

- Tip: Try their signature ale while enjoying the cozy setting.

Whisky in Scotland

Whisky (or Scotch) is an integral part of Scottish heritage. The country is divided into whisky regions Speyside, Islay, and the Highlands each known for distinct flavors and characteristics.

Glenfiddich Distillery, Dufftown: One of the most famous distilleries, offering tours and tastings.

- Address: Dufftown, Moray, AB55 4DH
- Opening Hours: 10:00 AM - 5:00 PM
- Price: Tours from £10.00

Ardbeg Distillery, Islay: A must-visit for peat whisky lovers, offering tours and tastings.

- Address: Port Ellen, Isle of Islay PA42 7EA
- Opening Hours: 10:00 AM - 5:00 PM
- Price: Tours from £12.00

The Macallan, Speyside: A luxurious distillery offering exceptional tasting experiences.

- Address: Craigellachie, Moray AB38 9RX
- Opening Hours: 10:00 AM - 5:00 PM

- Price: Tours from £15.00

Whisky-tasting festivals like the Spirit of Speyside Whisky Festival are held annually. Expect to sample a variety of whiskies, with opportunities to meet distillers and explore Scotland's whisky-making heritage.

FESTIVALS AND EVENTS YOU CAN'T-MISS

The United Kingdom is home to a vibrant mix of festivals and events, ranging from world-renowned music festivals to centuries-old traditions. Whether you're planning to dance to live music, immerse yourself in culture, or experience the thrill of a sporting event, this chapter will help you navigate the best of the UK's celebrations. With tips on dates, ticketing, transport, and accommodation, you'll be well-prepared to enjoy the UK's most iconic festivals and events.

Glastonbury Festival

Glastonbury is arguably the world's most famous music festival, attracting a diverse crowd of music lovers, festival-goers, and free spirits. Held in Pilton, Somerset, it's a magical five-day experience filled with live music, theater, circus acts, and more. Famous for its eclectic mix of music, from rock and pop to electronic and world music, Glastonbury offers something for everyone.

- Dates: Annually, typically the last weekend in June.
- Ticketing: Tickets sell out quickly, so planning is essential. The early bird sale opens months in advance, and there is a resale option in the spring. Sign up for updates and be prepared for the mad rush when tickets go live.

- What to Expect: From the iconic Pyramid Stage to the smaller, intimate venues, you'll find every genre imaginable. Past performances have included Beyoncé, Radiohead, Kendrick Lamar, and The Cure. Don't miss out on hidden gems and up-and-coming acts across the festival grounds.

- Camping Tips: Prepare for basic facilities. Consider booking a glamping option if you want extra comfort. Bring wellies, waterproofs, and a portable charger!

- Accommodation: Nearby towns like Glastonbury and Shepton Mallet offer B&Bs and campsites, but these fill up fast, so book early.

- Travel Tips: Bristol or Bath are the nearest major cities with train connections to the Pylle or Glastonbury Festival site. Expect heavy crowds and a long walk from the train station to the festival site.

Edinburgh Fringe Festival

The Edinburgh Fringe Festival is the world's largest arts festival, running for over three weeks every August. It's a celebration of creativity, with thousands of performances in genres such as theatre, comedy, music, and dance taking place across hundreds of venues in the city.

- Dates: August (typically the first three weeks).

- Ticket Booking: Shows at the Fringe are often affordable, but they can sell out fast. Book tickets early through the Edinburgh Fringe website. You can also buy tickets on-site, but you may face long lines.

- What to Expect: Over 50,000 performances and 3,000 shows! Comedy is a highlight, but you'll also find cutting-edge theater, dance performances, cabaret, and more. Don't miss the free street performances, where international artists showcase their talents.

- Top Shows: Keep an eye on the Fringe Programme for popular shows and recommendations. Past performances have featured legends like John Cleese and Stephen Fry.

- Where to Stay: Edinburgh gets very crowded during the Fringe. Booking accommodation well in advance is essential, especially if you want to stay in the city center. Consider staying in Leith or New Town for a quieter experience.

- Food & Drink: Enjoy the buzzing Royal Mile or pop into one of the many quirky pop-up cafes and bars around town.

Notting Hill Carnival

The Notting Hill Carnival is Europe's largest street festival, celebrating the vibrant culture of the Caribbean. Every

August Bank Holiday, the streets of Notting Hill, London, come alive with live music, colorful parades, and delicious food.

- Dates: Last weekend in August (Sunday and Monday).

- Parade Routes: The parade winds through Notting Hill, from Westbourne Park to Ladbroke Grove. Arrive early to grab a spot along the route.

- Cultural Experiences: Expect pulsating sounds of calypso, reggae, soca, and steel bands, as well as vibrant costumes, dancers, and performers. The Carnival also celebrates Afro-Caribbean history and culture.

- Food: Enjoy Jerk chicken, roti, goat curry, and other Caribbean specialties from street vendors.

- Family-Friendly Events: The Children's Day Parade takes place on Sunday, offering a more family-friendly atmosphere.

- Nightlife: The festival continues after dark with massive street parties. Be cautious, as these can get crowded and rowdy.

- Travel Tips: Tube stations such as Ladbroke Grove and Westbourne Park are the closest, but expect significant crowds and delays. Plan to arrive early or consider using local buses.

Hogmanay in Edinburgh

Hogmanay (New Year's Eve) in Edinburgh is a spectacular event, drawing crowds from around the world to celebrate the arrival of the new year. The festivities include live music, fireworks, a torchlight procession, and a massive street party.

- Dates: December 31.

Main Events:

- Torchlight Procession: The festivities start with a torchlight procession through the city, leading to Calton Hill for a magnificent view of the city and fireworks.

- Street Party: The main event is the Edinburgh Street Party, where revelers fill the streets for live music, dancing, and revelry. It's one of the biggest New Year's Eve celebrations in the world.

- Midnight Fireworks: The iconic fireworks display takes place over Edinburgh Castle, with thousands of people gathering on Princes Street for the best views.

- Ceilidh Dance: A traditional Scottish dance that invites everyone to join in the fun.

- Accommodation: Edinburgh gets busy, so book your hotel well in advance.
- Travel Tips: Check public transport schedules, as many services end earlier, and taxis can be hard to find. Wear warm clothes it's cold in December!

New Year's Eve Around the UK

- London Fireworks: The famous fireworks display along the Thames is a major attraction. The best views are from Westminster Bridge or the London Eye.
- Glasgow and Manchester: Both cities host vibrant celebrations with live music and fireworks. Check out George Square in Glasgow or Albert Square in Manchester for the best party atmosphere.

Sporting Events

Wimbledon

Wimbledon is the pinnacle of tennis, attracting top players and global audiences. It's not just about the sport; the event is a British cultural institution.

- Dates: Late June to early July.

- Ticketing: Tickets for Wimbledon are hard to come by but can be purchased via the official Wimbledon website or through a lottery system.

- What to Wear: Wimbledon has a famous all-white dress code for players, but visitors can wear smart casual attire. Don't forget your sunscreen!

- Key Matches: Watch top players like Novak Djokovic and Serena Williams compete for the grand prize.

- Accommodation: The nearest hotels are in South West London, but they book up fast. Try staying in Richmond or Putney for easier access.

- Transport: Wimbledon is accessible via Southfields Underground Station or Wimbl

- edon Station.

Rugby Matches

- Six Nations Championship: The rugby tournament involves the UK's top teams (England, Wales, Scotland, and Ireland) and is held every February and March.

- Key Matches: The England vs. Scotland game at Twickenham Stadium is a must-watch.

- Rugby World Cup: Held every four years, it's a global event with matches across the UK. Tickets can be purchased through the official tournament website.

Football Matches

- Premier League Matches: Attend iconic matches like Manchester United vs. Liverpool at Old Trafford or Arsenal vs. Tottenham in the North London Derby.

UNITED KINGDOM TRAVEL GUIDE

- FA Cup: The oldest football competition, the FA Cup final at Wembley Stadium is a must-see for football fans.

Christmas Markets

Winter Wonderland, Hyde Park: Experience an enchanting Christmas market, ice skating, and a funfair in London.

- Dates: November - January.
- Best Treats: Mulled wine, roasted chestnuts, and hand-made crafts.

Edinburgh Christmas Market: Wander through historic East Princes Street Gardens, where you can shop for festive treats and gifts.

Royal Events

- Changing of the Guard: Watch this iconic ceremony at Buckingham Palace.

- Royal Ascot: A prestigious horse race event in June.

- State Opening of Parliament: A royal procession marking the opening of the British Parliament.

TIPS FOR FIRST-TIME TRAVELERS

Embarking on your first trip to the United Kingdom is an exciting adventure. To help you make the most of your visit, this chapter provides essential tips on navigating the UK, understanding local etiquette, staying safe, and avoiding common tourist traps. Whether you're in London for the first time or exploring the Scottish Highlands, these practical tips will ensure you have a smooth and enjoyable trip.

Staying Safe and Dealing with Emergencies

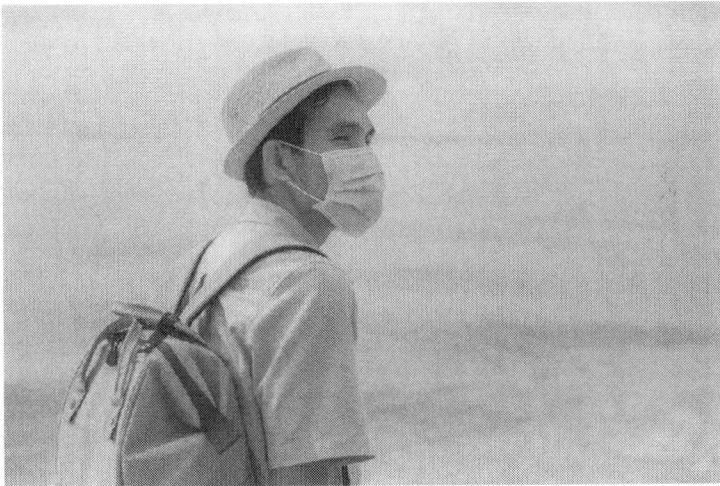

Staying Safe

The UK is generally a safe country to visit, but like any destination, it's important to stay vigilant.

- Avoid Common Scams: Watch out for pickpockets, especially in crowded tourist areas such as Covent

Garden or Piccadilly Circus. Always use official taxis or trusted rideshare services like Uber.

- Public Transport: The London Underground and buses are safe, but be aware of your belongings, particularly in busy stations or on late-night trains.
- Stay in Well-Lit Areas: If you're out after dark, stick to well-lit areas and avoid isolated places.

Emergency Numbers

In case of an emergency, dial 999 for the police, ambulance, or fire services. Keep a list of local hospitals or emergency services near your accommodation, just in case.

Travel Insurance

Always invest in comprehensive travel insurance to cover potential medical emergencies, trip cancellations, or lost luggage. Companies like Allianz, World Nomads, or InsureandGo offer plans tailored for international travelers.

Avoiding Tourist Traps

To steer clear of overpriced tourist traps, consider these tips:

- Skip Overcrowded Attractions: Popular spots like the London Eye or Madame Tussauds are always crowded and expensive. Instead, visit free museums like the Victoria and Albert Museum or the National Gallery.

- Dining Away from Tourist Areas: Restaurants in major tourist districts tend to be overpriced. Seek out local favorites for a more authentic and affordable experience. Apps like TripAdvisor can help you find hidden gems.

Hidden Gems and Local Favorites

The UK is full of lesser-known attractions that offer an authentic taste of local life:

- The Seven Dials (London): This charming area, nestled in Covent Garden, features independent boutiques, cozy cafes, and a quieter, more relaxed atmosphere than other touristy areas.

- Portobello Road Market (London): A great alternative to crowded shopping streets, this market offers vintage clothing, antiques, and delicious street food.

- The Cotswolds (England): A picturesque region with quaint villages like Bourton-on-the-Water and Stow-on-the-Wold, perfect for a peaceful escape from the hustle and bustle.

Locals are the best source of recommendations for hidden gems. Don't hesitate to ask for their tips on where to eat, shop, or explore. You can also consult apps like Yelp for real-time, local insights.

Pacing Your Trip

Avoid the temptation to over-schedule your trip. While it's tempting to see everything, it's better to focus on a few key attractions and allow time to explore on your own.

- Balance Major Attractions and Relaxation: For example, spend a full day visiting the museums in South Kensington, and then take a stroll around nearby Hyde Park or Notting Hill.

- Take Time to Explore: After ticking off iconic attractions, wander through neighborhoods like Greenwich or Hampstead for a more laid-back experience.

Relaxation Tips

- Remember to take a break and enjoy some downtime. Try:

- Afternoon Tea: Visit a traditional tearoom in Bath or York for a relaxing and quintessentially British experience.

- Botanical Gardens: Explore places like Kew Gardens in London or the Royal Botanic Garden in Edinburgh for a tranquil escape.

Immerse yourself in British culture. Attend a local festival, try regional foods, or enjoy an afternoon in a local pub. Whether it's a quiet evening in a traditional pub or catching a play in London's West End, these experiences will help you connect with the country on a deeper level.

SAMPLE ITINERARIES FOR

DIFFERENT TRAVELERS

3-Day London Adventure

Day 1: Royal and Iconic London

- Morning: Start your adventure with a visit to Buckingham Palace to see the Changing of the Guard, then head over to Westminster Abbey, a

UNESCO World Heritage site and one of London's most iconic landmarks. Finish your morning by taking a short walk to the Houses of Parliament and Big Ben.

- Afternoon: After lunch, take a ride on the London Eye for panoramic views of the city. Once you've soaked in the views, make your way to the Tate Modern, where you can explore world-class contemporary art exhibitions.

- Evening: Conclude your day in Covent Garden, known for its charming cobbled streets and vibrant street performances. Enjoy dinner at a nearby restaurant, whether it's a cozy British pub or a trendy bistro.

- Practical Tip: Use an Oyster card for easy access to London's public transport network. Book tickets in advance for the London Eye and West End shows to avoid long queues.

Day 2: Historic London and Hidden Gems

- Morning: Begin your day with a visit to the Tower of London. Explore the Crown Jewels and hear about the castle's fascinating history. Afterward, walk across the iconic Tower Bridge for stunning views of the Thames.

- Afternoon: Head to the British Museum to admire its incredible collection of ancient artifacts, including the Rosetta Stone. Next, take a stroll through Leadenhall Market, a historic covered market known for its vibrant architecture and unique shops.

- Evening: Explore Soho for dinner, where you'll find a bustling nightlife scene and a diverse range of restaurants, bars, and pubs.

Day 3: Markets, Parks, and Culture

- Morning: Start the day at Borough Market, London's most famous food market, where you can sample fresh produce, artisanal cheeses, and street food. Afterward, take a walk along the South Bank for scenic views of the River Thames.

- Afternoon: Spend your afternoon exploring the Victoria and Albert Museum, a treasure trove of decorative arts and design. For a bit of relaxation, take a break at Hyde Park or Kensington Gardens, two of London's most peaceful green spaces.

- Evening: End your London adventure with a West End show in the theatre district. Be sure to book tickets ahead to secure the best seats.

- Practical Tip: Consider staying in central London to maximize your time. Areas like Covent Garden, Soho, and South Bank offer easy access to major attractions.

4 Days of Nature, History, and Culture

Day 1: Edinburgh's Historic Heart

- Morning: Begin your journey at Edinburgh Castle, perched on Castle Rock. Explore its museums and enjoy panoramic views of the city.

- Afternoon: Walk along the Royal Mile, a historic street lined with shops, cafes, and street performers. Don't miss St Giles' Cathedral and Holyrood Palace at the end of the Mile.

- Evening: Have dinner in the Grassmarket area, known for its traditional Scottish pubs and historic charm.

Day 2: Exploring Nature and the City

- Morning: Hike up Arthur's Seat, an extinct volcano that offers stunning views of Edinburgh and the surrounding hills. It's a relatively easy hike and a great way to see the city from above.

- Afternoon: Visit the National Museum of Scotland to delve into the country's history, then unwind in the tranquil Princes Street Gardens.

- Evening: Attend a Scottish ceilidh (folk dance) or enjoy a whisky tasting experience in one of the city's many whisky bars.

Day 3: Day Trip to Stirling

- Morning: Take a short trip to Stirling, where you can explore Stirling Castle, a key site in Scotland's history. The castle played a crucial role in the Wars of Independence.

- Afternoon: Visit the Wallace Monument, dedicated to the Scottish hero William Wallace, and enjoy scenic views of the surrounding countryside.

- Evening: Return to Edinburgh for a relaxing evening at a local pub, sampling some traditional Scottish food.

Day 4: Highlands Adventure

- Day Trip: Head into the Scottish Highlands for a scenic drive, visiting Loch Ness and the town of Inverness. The area offers breathtaking landscapes and a chance to learn about the legends of Loch Ness.

- Return to Edinburgh: Finish your trip by heading back to Edinburgh in the evening.

- Practical Tip: Renting a car is recommended for the Highlands. If you prefer not to drive, you can book day trips from Edinburgh to the surrounding areas via train or bus.

5 Days of Coastal Beauty and Welsh Heritage

Day 1: Cardiff

- Morning: Start at Cardiff Castle, a magnificent fortress in the heart of the city. Explore its stunning interiors and gardens.

- Afternoon: Visit the National Museum Cardiff to see an impressive collection of art and archaeology. Stroll around Bute Park for a relaxing afternoon.

- Evening: Head to Cardiff Bay, a vibrant area filled with shops, restaurants, and waterfront views. Enjoy dinner at one of the bay's many eateries.

Day 2: Brecon Beacons National Park

- Morning: Take a trip to Brecon Beacons National Park, where you can hike through breathtaking mountains and see stunning waterfalls.
- Afternoon: Explore the market town of Brecon and visit Brecon Cathedral.
- Evening: Return to Cardiff for a relaxing evening at a local pub or restaurant.

Day 3: Pembrokeshire Coast National Park

- Day Trip: Drive to Pembrokeshire to explore its scenic coastline. Visit Barafundle Bay, one of the most beautiful beaches in Wales, and the charming town of Tenby.

- Evening: Return to Cardiff or stay overnight in Pembrokeshire for a slower-paced evening.

Day 4: Snowdonia National Park

- Morning: Take the scenic train up Snowdon, the highest peak in Wales, for spectacular views. Alternatively, you can hike up if you're up for the challenge.

- Afternoon: Visit Betws-y-Coed, a picturesque village nestled in the forests of Snowdonia. Enjoy a leisurely walk and a cup of tea in one of its cozy cafes.

- Evening: Stay overnight in the area, enjoying local Welsh food in a traditional pub.

Day 5: Conwy and Caernarfon Castles

- Morning: Visit Conwy Castle, a UNESCO World Heritage site, and explore the medieval town walls.

- Afternoon: Head to Caernarfon to see its impressive castle, a landmark of Welsh heritage.

- Evening: Return to Cardiff, wrapping up your Welsh adventure.

- Practical Tip: Scenic drives along the coast offer incredible views. Consider guided tours for remote areas and book accommodations in advance for quieter regions.

Notes

Manufactured by Amazon.ca
Bolton, ON